ALL-AMERICAN INDIAN

THIS FIGHT IS YOUR FIGHT

The Battle to Save America from the Elites Who Think They Know Better

DR. SHIVA AYYADURAI

Award-Winning Inventor of *Email*, *EchoMail* & *CytoSolve*

To Woody Guthrie

Printed in the United States of America.

First Edition, 2017.

ISBN 978-0-9985049-2-6

General Interactive, LLC
Publishing Division
701 Concord Ave.
Cambridge, MA 02138
www.generalinteractive.com

All proceeds from the sale of this book go to Innovation Corps, a 501 (c) not-for-profit project dedicated to supporting youth innovation.
www.innovationcorps.org

Contents

Introduction

Let's begin with a basic observation about how things really work. I'm a scientist and an engineer, so knowing how things work in the world is very important to me, and there's one principle of Nature that's absolutely fundamental. It's the principle that Nature -- the greatest of all engineers -- has used to construct literally everything.

In one word, it's the principle of ***decentralization***. Nature does not intend for any one species, or any one country, or any one person, or even any one organ of the human body to have monopoly control of power or wisdom or health. To give just one example, the brain is not the sole repository of what we call thought. If the brain "thinks," so does the stomach and the small intestine. As a Ph.D. in biological engineering, I can speak with authority about this.

It's taken science a long time to grasp the principle of decentralization, and in other areas of life it's taking even longer. In our government, for example, there's a whole class of career politicians who believe -- despite what Nature's example teaches us.-- that power should be centralized.

And where should power be centralized? In themselves, of course. They should make the decisions because they believe they're smarter. They should have the power (and money too) because they know better.

But I know that YOU know better, just as the Founding Fathers knew that that "we the people" collectively are wiser than any person or small group individually. At its core, centralization is human greed. Decentralization is Natural Law.

With the wisdom of decentralization -- that one key word -- as a guiding principle, I want to begin this book by looking at three other words that have been very important to me personally, and that are now the subject of intense debate across our country:

- *Immigration*
- *Education*
- *Innovation*

Those words are the real foundations of America's past. They need to be the foundations of America's future.

But it won't happen by itself. I can say that with confidence because immigration, education, and innovation have been the central experiences of my life. I know the hard work that was required from my parents, my teachers, and from myself as well.

I also know how fulfilling that work has been. With that in mind, this book will invite you

-- and challenge you -- to recognize what immigration, education, and innovation mean for our nation. And also what those words can mean in your own life, starting right now.

My family legally immigrated to America when I was seven years old. My parents chose to leave India because of the limitations that Indian society placed on the lower caste population, regardless of the talents that population might possess. In contrast, they saw America as a place of meritocracy --- where hard work and ability would be rewarded. It was the same vision that inspired many thousands of families since the United States was founded.

That's the literal and historical definition of immigration. But the deeper meaning of immigration is beyond that definition.

Whenever you let go of worn-out ways of thinking, whenever you stop accepting limits that others are imposing on you, whenever you enter a new landscape in your career or in your personal life, that's immigration.

When you immigrate to a place of new opportunity, the next step is knowing how to take full advantage of it. That means education. That can mean graduating from high school, or it can mean getting an advanced degree.

But, as with immigration, there is also a broader definition of education. The Latin root of the word is "ex ducere," which means "to lead out of." Education is simply a journey out of ignorance to deeper understanding. We can and should continue that journey throughout our lives. That means continuing to expand our knowledge intellectually, emotionally, spiritually, and politically.

Innovation is the natural outgrowth of education. Sometimes it's finding new and better ways of doing the things you've always done. It can also be discovering entirely new things you want to do. An innovation can be a physical object, or a new idea, or an insight for positive change. It can be finding a faster route for driving to our job, or it can be leaving your present job for a better one, or it can be developing a product that creates an entirely new industry. That's what happened when the first automobiles were built, and when the first planes flew, and when the first computers booted up. And there are more great innovations waiting to happen.

In this book I will share my experiences with immigration, education, and innovation. You'll see the practical lessons I've learned -- lessons that you can apply in your own life. As you apply those lessons, you'll become a revolutionary in the truest sense of the word.

Being a revolutionary doesn't mean violence. It means seeing the truth, refusing to accept anything less than the truth, and being willing to fight for the truth in every area of your life.

Being a revolutionary means recognizing the resistance and hostility that you'll encounter from the Establishment powers, and the Elites who think they know better, and who will attempt to attack and delegitimize any creation or innovation that doesn't come from the their control or purview.

Creative people, genuine change makers, have always faced that resistance and they always will. They have had to take personal accountability for their dreams and their vision. This was a pre-requisite before coming together in any Union. As innovators and revolutionaries, while we're in this together, each of must internalize this struggle and recognize that this is "*your* fight" as an individual first, and *then* as a People, which is exactly how it should be. That's why the United States Constitution begins with these all-important words:

We The People of the United States in Order to form a more perfect Union...

Part One

Be the Light

Chapter One

Bombay

My mother and I -- both of us -- almost died during childbirth. My father had to go to his work in a factory. He left the hospital thinking we were going to die. We survived but my life was precarious. Because of my mother's condition, I was not breast-fed and was given goat's milk instead.

This happened in Bombay, the city now officially known as Mumbai but still called Bombay by many people who live there. That's where I came to love chaos and diversity. There were so many religions, classes, castes, cultures, races, colors and languages. There were new buildings made of glass, metal, and steel side-by-side with huts made of twigs, grass, old tires, straw, mud, and wire.

Our neighbors were Jews, Christians, Hindus, Muslims, Jains and Zoroastrians. Sadhus and yogis meditated along the road. Transvestites, transsexuals, gays, straight men, women, and children walked hand in hand. Being multi-lingual was the rule, not the exception. At home, we spoke Tamil and, in school, English. On the streets we spoke Hindi. With friends we spoke Marathi.

The streets were full of extreme contrasts. Many people walked. Others pulled rickshaws. Bicycles and Mercedes rode side by side. Beggars crawled. Boeing 747s roared. The smells of roasting peanuts, scrumptious curries, exhausts from diesel trucks, roadside pooris, and cow dung, were all in the air.

The outdoor markets offered sugarcane juice, goat brains, 24-karat jewelry, jackfruits, radios, malas, incense, parrots, and fragrant spices. Women in colorful gold, blue and red saris strode by women decked out in the latest Italian fashion. Men wearing traditional Nehru jackets, white dhotis, and hats conversed with businessmen in Brooks Brothers suits.

The yard behind our apartment in Bombay was like a prehistoric jungle with cobras, parrots, and other wildlife. It was a place of excitement, wonder, and discovery. Above all, it was a place of freedom.

But I also saw the realities of the society into which I had been born. I was non-Brahmin, a lower-caste, "an untouchable," -- as if that were a different species or order of being.

Once after playing soccer, I went to my "friend's" house. His mother stopped me at the front door referring to me as "Shudra," and would not allow me to into her home. She then

ALL-AMERICAN INDIAN

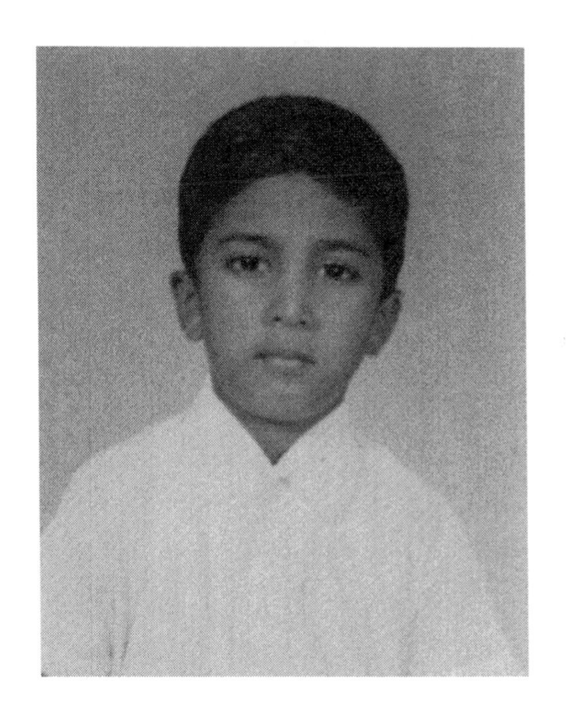

had me stand outside and gave me water in a distinctly different cup than her son's. That incident stung and still remains within me.

When I asked my mother why that happened, she shared with me that in India the word "Shudra," the equivalent of "Nigger," was used to refer to us. She told me about these and other insults she had endured as a young child. When she went to fetch water at the local well, the upper caste women would all run away while yelling "Shoo Shoo Shudra" to demand she leave.

Within that environment, I wanted to know why such injustice existed, and what I could do to fight it. One day, I felt very inspired when a friend of my father came to our house and told me stories of revolutionaries fighting on behalf of the poor. I immediately felt united with their cause, and my father's friend called me a five-year-old Communist. I had no idea what that word meant, but if it meant someone who was seeking truth, freedom and justice, than I connected with them.

It would, however, take me many years to know the difference between those who sought change by centralizing power within the few who "knew better" and those who sought change by decentralizing power to the individual, believing in the innate and divine spark within each human to forge their own destiny through hard work and ingenuity.

Chapter Two

A Different World

In the summers, the scenes radically changed. Bombay disappeared. A forty-eight hour journey on a coal-powered caboose train took me to the remote village of Muhavur, located in the south Indian state of Tamil Nadu. Bombay was a frenzied city of the present and the future, but this was the land of my ancestors, timeless and serene. It was an emerald landscape of rice and cotton fields, mango and coconut groves, mountains and streams.

In Muhavur there was minimal electricity, no running water, and a few scattered phone booths -- it brought one to a different reality. This was the village of my grandparents, hardworking farmers, who tilled the fields, awoke at 4AM and slept at dusk. They lived simply, devoted to land and God.

Their home was a small two-story building. Each morning before sunrise my grandmother drew beautiful *kolams* on the entrance to the home.

Her name was Chinnathai. With milled white rice flour that flowed through her hands, like sand passing through an hourglass, she made those intricate geometric designs. They were visions from her mind's eye translated onto the red earth. The designs were said to evoke the Gods, and transform the consciousness of everyone who saw them.

Entering that home, it was impossible to ignore the kolam. They were a reminder that you

ALL-AMERICAN INDIAN

had come to a special place. Two doors of solid teak opened onto a 10- by 12-foot space thatserved as a living room, a dining room and a sleeping room. Beyond was the kitchen, where something was always cooking. The fragrance of cumin, ginger, cardamom, red pepper, and freshly grated coconut filled the air.

On all four walls of the living room hung pictures of great deities and heroes such as Shiva, my namesake, who destroyed, created and transformed; Rama, the virtuous and noble hero of the Ramayana; Devi, the mother Goddess; Parvathi, wife and consort of Shiva; Ganesha, the elephant headed one who removed obstacles; Jesus, God's avatar and the Savior of mankind; Saraswati, the Goddess of knowledge; Lakshmi, the Goddess of wealth, and many others. The smell of subtle incense and Vibbuthi, holy ash, was always in the air.

My favorite was Muruga, the deity who graced the small altar, and was known as the teacher of teachers or guru of gurus. He was the warrior God who, like Archangel Michael, defeated the Asuras (devils) that were overcoming the Devas (angels) in heaven. And, he was also the God of medicine, who brought Siddha, India's traditional system of healing, to Earth. Muruga's vehicle for transport was the peacock; and, in that altar, above his picture hung a beautiful single peacock feather.

Chapter Three

The Healer

Chinnathai knew the ancient arts, she could channel spirits, she was known to be clairvoyant, she had knowledge of the great herbs and medicines for nearly any ailment, and she would do rituals and mantras to heal those who requested her help.

Even as a small child I was fascinated by the depth of her knowledge about so many amazing things -- especially since I knew that she had no conventional education. But this was more than just interesting to me. Being around my grandmother motivated me to be a person like her. It didn't matter where she lived or how much money she had. She knew who she was and what she could accomplish, and everyone who saw her immediately knew that too.

Chinnathai was the youngest of sixteen children, and the only daughter. Her arms were marked with ancient tattoos. She had a nose ring. Her hair was pitch black, she chewed tobacco and betel leaf. Her face was like the earth, dark and hues of red, with eyes that extended to the beyond and lines that marked her journeys of many life times.

Along with working in the fields for sixteen hours a day, she was a healer in the traditional Indian system of health called Siddha. She could literally tell what was going on in a person's body simply by looking at that person's face. In India this ancient practice known is known as *Samudrika Lakshanam,* the art of face reading.

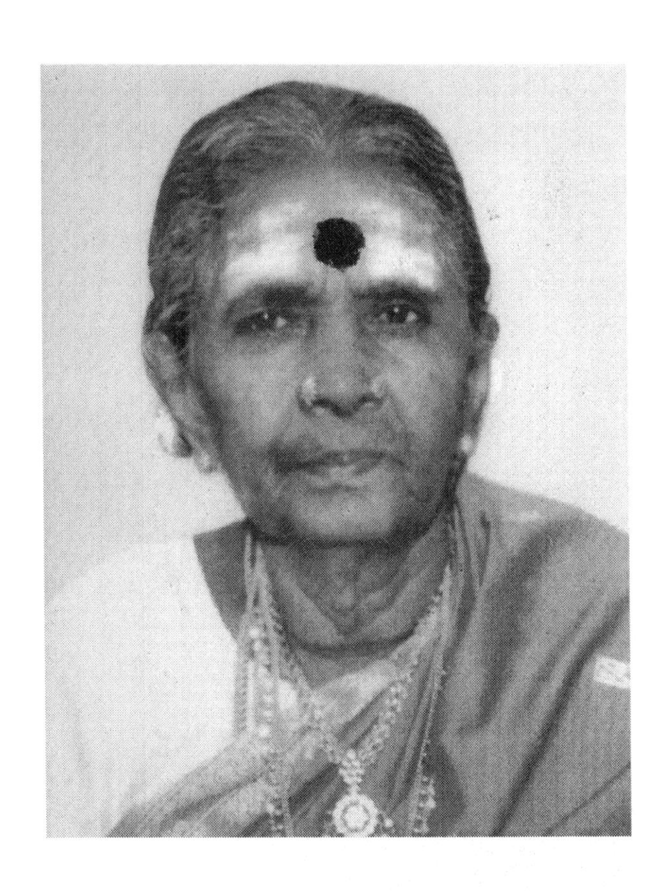

Then she could provide a healing prescription -- it could include massage, or yoga, or a variety of herbs -- that addressed not only specific symptoms, but also the person's unique and individual identity. It was truly a holistic approach. It was also in sync with modern systems theory that I would later learn at MIT, although I of course didn't know it at the time.

Every day, people came to Chinnathai asking for help with their health. On weekends, long lines extended from her door. I was amazed by her ability to diagnose someone's problem by simply observing his or her face. She had learned powers of diagnosis from yogis, monks, and the sages known as Siddhars.

She shared with me how the Siddhars believed that the entire cosmos including the smallest particle to the largest universe were connected by consciousness and energy. The face was just a mirror of our entire body, and areas on the face were connected to organs, emotions and mind.

Chapter Four

The Siddhars

The practitioner of Siddha connected the dots, based on centuries of patiently observing patterns. These are the kind of insights that modern systems biology hopes to develop by interconnecting chains of molecular interactions. This is something I would later do, with one of my inventions CytoSolve, during my Ph.D. research at MIT.

The importance of Siddha has nothing to do with sentimental ideas about the past or the charm of so-called primitive beliefs. In fact, the exact opposite is true. What's fascinating about

Siddha is how contemporary it is. As Ph.D. scientist, I immediately recognized how Siddha anticipated the logical principles of modern systems biology. Superstitious beliefs such as the caste system or the subjugation of women had no place in Siddha. My grandmother was sought after as a healer in the Indian countryside for the same reason that Americans seek out the best doctors and hospitals. It was simply because her insights were accurate, and her treatments were effective. What could be more modern than that?

I remember how carefully she would observe someone's face, seeing so much that others would overlook. Her powers of observation, without the aid of any instruments, were incredible. She saw colorings, marks, moles, lines, locations and asymmetries. Her mind and training then connected these features to areas of imbalances in the body. After determining the issues, she would then prescribe a treatment.

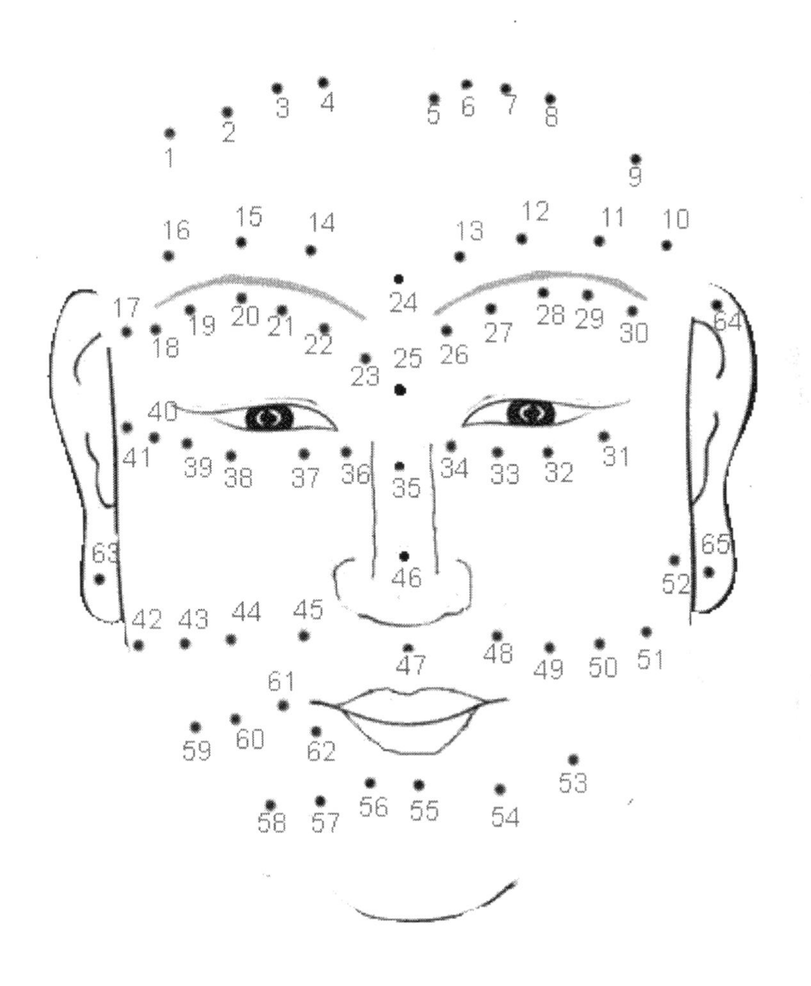
1
2
3
4
5
6
7
8
9
10
11
12
13
14
15
16
17
18
19
20
21
22
23
24
25
26
27
28
29
30
31
32
33
34
35
36
37
38
39
40
41
42
43
44
45
46
47
48
49
50
51
52
53
54
55
56
57
58
59
60
61
62
63
64
65

It was easy for her to spot a person with a diseased liver, for example, by noticing a vertical line on the person's forehead. Many years later, when my father was once admitted to the hospital, even after a week of tests the doctors were not able to make any conclusive diagnosis. When I came to the hospital, I knew by observing my father's face that the problem was his thyroid. I took him home and gave him a mixture of herbs specifically suited to relieve the stress on that organ. Within a few days he was up and around.

Chapter Five

Coming to America

My parents, Meenakshi and Vellayappa Ayyadurai, worked hard to get an education at a time when people of our background had a low ceiling for advancement in India. So on December 2, 1970, my mother, sister and I left India to join my father, who had gone a year earlier, with $75.00 in his pocket. In fact, we left India exactly on my seventh birthday. My father had moved us, his young wife and two small children, to the United States to pursue the American Dream.

Snow was falling as I got off the plane at John F. Kennedy Airport. I was wearing shorts. Somehow none of us anticipated that winter in

New York was going to be very different from Bombay. That was the first instance of the long learning curve we would encounter in the United States.

In 1970, the era of high technology in America was just beginning. Since my parents had training in engineering and mathematics, they were granted visas to enter America. But 1970 was also a bad year economically in America. There was a recession underway and the job my father had been offered didn't work out.

We first lived in Paterson, New Jersey, one of the poorest cities in the country. It was the period of long-haired hippies, bell bottoms, Black Power, and weed. Quite a scene, and in some ways it reminded me of Bombay. My father later found a job as a chemical engineer at Mennen Corporation in Morristown, and my mother was a systems analyst and mathematician at the

ALL-AMERICAN INDIAN

University of Medicine and Dentistry of New Jersey (UMDNJ) in Newark. They worked endless hours to build a life for my sister and me.

After Paterson we moved to Clifton, and then to Lake Hiawatha, which was a turning point. One of my teachers was Mr. Roth, who had been in the navy off the shores of Japan when the atomic bomb was dropped on Hiroshima. During the summers he often brought my sister and me to his home, since my parents were always working. Mr. Roth introduced me to his son David, who was good at math and music. In David, I saw the opportunity to be both an artist and a scientist, which would later compel my pursuit of education in not only engineering and science education but also in visual design, graphics and animation at the MIT Media Laboratory.

With each advance in their careers, my parents moved the family to a new neighborhood with a better public school system. This was their

AYYADURAI'S FOUR POINT THEOREM

Shiva Ayyadurai
Student
Livingston High School
Livingston, N.J. 07039

(In the course of an independent study project Shiva Ayyadurai, a Junior at Livingston High School, became interested in Ptolemy's Theorem. He was at the time studying Vector Geometry and made an attempt to prove this theorem by vector methods. Shiva did not accomplish this yet but he did run across the following interesting result. -- Ed.)

In the course of investigating Ptolemy's Theorem, I encountered a most interesting relationship. Ptolemy's Theorem states that in a cyclic quadrilateral, the sum of the products of the magnitudes of the opposite sides is equal to the product of the magnitudes of the diagonals. By using vector methods, I discovered that the Dot products of the diagonals is equal to the sum of the Dot products of the opposite sides; furthermore, this relationship is true for all quadrilaterals, and, more generally, it is applicable to any four points in space. A Dot product is a scalar quantity, obtained when two vectors are multiplied.

<u>Proof</u>:

In any quadrilateral, the sum of the Dot products of the opposite sides is equal to the Dot products of the diagonals. Refer to Fig. 1.

$$\vec{AC} = \vec{AP} + \vec{PC}$$
$$\vec{BD} = \vec{BP} + \vec{PD}$$
$$\vec{AC}\cdot\vec{BD} = (\vec{AP} + \vec{PC})\cdot(\vec{BP} + \vec{PD})$$

$$\vec{AB} = \vec{AP} - \vec{BP}$$
$$\vec{CD} = \vec{PD} - \vec{PC}$$
$$\vec{AB}\cdot\vec{CD} = (\vec{AP} - \vec{BP})\cdot(\vec{PD} - \vec{PC})$$
$$= \vec{AP}\cdot\vec{PD} - \vec{AP}\cdot\vec{PC} - \vec{BP}\cdot\vec{PD} + \vec{BP}\cdot\vec{PC}$$

$$\vec{AD} = \vec{AP} + \vec{PD}$$
$$\vec{BC} = \vec{BP} + \vec{PC}$$
$$\vec{AD}\cdot\vec{BC} = (\vec{AP} + \vec{PD})\cdot(\vec{BP} + \vec{PC})$$
$$= \vec{AP}\cdot\vec{BP} + \vec{AP}\cdot\vec{PC} + \vec{PD}\cdot\vec{BP} + \vec{PD}\cdot\vec{PC}$$

Add the Dot products of $\vec{AB}\cdot\vec{CD}$ and $\vec{AD}\cdot\vec{BC}$:

$$\vec{AB}\cdot\vec{CD} + \vec{AD}\cdot\vec{BC} = \vec{AP}\cdot\vec{PD} + \vec{AP}\cdot\vec{BP} + \vec{BP}\cdot\vec{PC} + \vec{PD}\cdot\vec{PC}$$
$$= \vec{AP}\cdot(\vec{PD} + \vec{BP}) + \vec{PC}\cdot(\vec{BP} + \vec{PD})$$
$$= (\vec{AP} + \vec{PC})\cdot(\vec{PD} + \vec{BP})$$
$$= \vec{AC}\cdot\vec{BD}$$
$$\therefore \vec{AB}\cdot\vec{CD} + \vec{AD}\cdot\vec{BC} = \vec{AC}\cdot\vec{BD}$$

As I have stated before, this theorem is valid for any four points in space. They can be collinear, coplanar, or non-coplanar. In fact, the points need not necessarily be distinct.

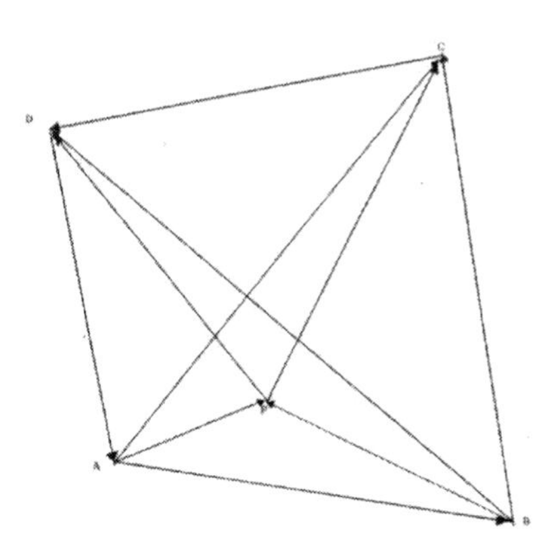

Note: Point P may be selected anywhere in space, to prove the theorem. Since no restriction is placed on the other four points; A, B, C, D. This theorem is applicable to any four points in space.

way of exercising "school choice." By the time I was 13, it had become clear to both my parents and teachers that I showed great intellectual promise, but was also becoming bored within the standard curriculum.

But, I wasn't a typical "nerd." I was motivated to do well in school but I was also very much into sports, especially baseball and soccer. I completed all the school's math courses, including calculus, by the ninth grade, and even published a paper in a mathematics journal as a teenager.

I did well in school for a very specific reason. I had been inspired by my grandmother and I wanted to learn medicine and healing. I had very practical goals.

Chapter Six

Seeing the Difference

During my first visit back to India to see my grandparents in 1975, I realized the stark contrast between life in rural India and life in the United States. It wasn't only the difference in income or housing. The lives of the people in Muhavur were incredibly simple, and based on a spiritual foundation. Material circumstances were secondary to spiritual well-being, provided that people knew how to create that spiritual well-being – which is exactly what my grandparents and many other people in South India had learned to do.

But being spiritual didn't mean being passive. In America there's a stereotype of the "nice" Indian who puts his hands together and bows, and meditates in the lotus position. That's not how it was in the Indian countryside. My grandmother taught me that a healer needed a warrior's attitude, with a desire to serve others and an understanding that being able to serve others was a gift from God.

She was the last of her sixteen siblings. She had adored her father, whom she described as Robin Hood. He would steal from the rich and give to the poor, and was beloved by all. I enjoyed hearing those stories, as well as the great epics of Indian gods and demons. Virtue and honor always overcame deceit and control.

She told me stories of the great Rama and how he fought the evil Ravana, who had stolen Sita, his beloved wife. Rama defeated Ravana and brought his wife home to safety. That great epic of the Ramayana, the valiant journey of Rama, and the bond between him and his devoted brother Lakshman, who would do anything for Rama, inspired in me a grand and uncompromising idealism for making the world a better place, fighting for justice, finding true love, and having devoted and loyal friendships.

Gossip was never allowed in Chinnathai's home. At night, I would sit at her feet, and she would tell me the ancient stories. After each one, I would ask her for the lesson from the story. What was its meaning? She would counsel me gently about the age-old truths of kindness, courage, and standing up for those who were less fortunate. She reminded me that we are ultimately Spirit, neither body nor mind. If we undertook right action, with honor, God's light would shine through our being, preparing us to be vehicles of great and noble deeds. And, "to Be the Light," was the purpose of life.

Life made sense in Muhavur. I could walk barefoot there, bathe in streams, watch cows going out to graze each morning, have fresh raw milk topped with cream, see where my food came from, know that Nature was in every corner and that even the barest essentials could be enough. At night, it was a wonder to walk through the narrow streets amid scents of the most amazing hot teas and coffee, people smiling, small wood fires burning, and looking up to see a thousand stars.

And the food, made with so much love and care, was always enlivening to the senses. Today, organic, non-GMO, and biodynamic foods are still a struggle for the average American to afford and access. But in Muhavur, in a small and seemingly poor village, people lived a totally organic and sustainable life that was one with nature. This was not some miracle. It was simply the norm.

During that visit, my grandparents introduced me to mantra meditation and visualization. They shared with me the immense power of these practices and made me promise that I would pursue these ancient practices with the right intention. They spent a great deal of time explaining to me that intention was everything.

Even the practices of yoga, meditation, and diet had to be pursued with the singular intention of purifying oneself to become more transparent to God's grace; otherwise, one could easily head down the path of darkness.

She told me that just because I meditated or did yoga or ate right, did not mean that I was a better person; in fact, one could end up becoming the exact opposite and manifest all the seven deadly sins.

When I left India after that visit, my grandparents came to the train station to see me off. All of us were in tears. As the grandson of Chinnathai, I made a promise to develop myself physically, mentally, and spiritually. I made a commitment to honor the lives of my grandparents and their way of being: a way of the land, pure and simple, whose values I would help to spread and perhaps one day heal the world.

I took with me that peacock feather that hung above the image of the great deity Muruga, a gift from my grandmother, to remind me of that promise to learn and excel so that one day I too could become a great healer like my grandmother --- and to Be the Light.

Part Two

The Invention of Email

Chapter Seven

A Quick Learner

I'll always be grateful for the commitment and sacrifices my parents made for my education. Our moves from one town to another were always intended to connect with the best public schools for my sister and me.

I had some amazing teachers in the New Jersey public school system. These were truly dedicated people and I have very clear memories of them even from the very early years. My third grade teacher, Ms. Hall, taught me the importance of detailed and descriptive writing. Mr. Roth, my sixth grade teacher, took time outside of class to teach me advanced imaginary numbers.

Mr. Sommer was an incredible teacher who let me depart from the standard curriculum so I could later finish calculus by ninth grade. He arranged for a special bus to take me to Livingston High School to take the twelfth grade calculus class. These teachers were dedicated to their students. Mr. Walker, my high school AP Chemistry teacher, who went on to win a national teaching award, held two other jobs in construction so he could put his kids through college. In retrospect, they taught me more than what I got from my MIT education.

Beyond my academic work, and side by side with my experiences in India, I was also an "All-American" kid. I had a paper route and a lawn mowing business. I was a Yankees fan. In high school, I was on the undefeated, state champion soccer team. I was also one of two students selected for the American Legion's

Jersey Boys State, the same program for which Bill Clinton was selected.

In the late 1970s, the Courant Institute for Mathematical Science at New York University (NYU) had started a new innovative program in which forty young students were invited to come to NYU to study computer programming. The program was created by a visionary professor, named Henry Mullish. He saw that software would be a primary need in the high tech revolution that was just beginning. He also took the initiative in preparing the next generation of students to meet that need. I was one of the invited students, and I learned six programming languages: COBOL, SNOBOL, FORTRAN, PL/1, BASIC and ARTSPK.

Getting to NYU from New Jersey involved taking buses and trains, starting at around five in the morning. My parents allowed me to make that trip because, like Professor Mullish, they saw that technology was the future.

I'd arrive in New York around seven in the morning, and then walk to the University through Washington Square Park, the colorful and sometimes threatening environment that was New York in those days. It was a twelve-hour per day program and it went on for eight weeks.

I was the youngest student, the only Indian, and I finished number one in the class.

Chapter Eight

Email – The System

When the NYU program ended I was bored by the idea of going back to high school. I was even thinking about dropping out. Fortunately my mom had gotten a degree in statistics in India at a time when it was very unusual, or even revolutionary, for a woman to do anything like that. She was working as a systems analyst at a small, three-campus medical school called the University of Medicine and Dentistry of New Jersey (UMDNJ).

My mother introduced me to a scientist named Dr. Swamy Laxminaraynan who had a large amount of data on sudden crib death of infants in their sleep, also known as sudden infant death syndrome (SIDS). He asked me to explore the data and develop artificial intelligence (AI) techniques to see if there was a correlation between infants' sleep patterns and crib death. This was my introduction to AI and pattern analysis of "Big Data."

Later this would become an important part of my career.

The results were later published as a scientific paper. This was very exciting and gratifying for me, since it was directly connected to my interest in medicine and healing. Inspired by my grandmother in India, I was on my chosen path.

Swamy Laxminaraynan was not the only contact my mother made for me, or even the most important. She also introduced me to Dr. Leslie P. Michelson, an experimental high-energy physicist, who became the Director of the

Laboratory Computer Network (LCN) at UMDNJ.

An internship for Dr. Michelson at his lab would provide me an opportunity to use my skills in math and science as well as my latest training from NYU in computer programming, among adult professionals in the field. Dr. Michelson took me on. He had to fight with the UMDNJ administration in order to bring in a high school student. In the same way, Ms. Stella Oleksiak, a incredible woman who had initiated an Independent Study program at Livingston High School (LHS), fought for and changed the rules on my behalf with the LHS superintendent's office, so I could go to Newark in the middle of the day.

Dr. Michelson's Lab was specializing in the use of computers for medicine, and scientific and data processing. At UMDNJ, as in the rest of the world, only technical people, computer systems operators, scientists and engineers, at that time, had access to and use for a computer.

I hoped Dr. Michelson would point me toward using my programming on a medical research project, but he had a different challenge in mind.

He asked me to translate the paper-based interoffice mail and memo system into an electronic form. The new system needed to be practical and easy to use.

Everyone from secretaries to CEOs should be able to quickly and reliably manage and process the interoffice memorandum in a digital format, and the final product needed to have all the features of the interoffice mail system: Inbox, Outbox, Folders, Address Book, Attachments, etc.

Users must be able to make a seamless, effortless transition from old-fashioned typewriters to computer terminals and keyboards. Although systems for exchanging

ALL-AMERICAN INDIAN

simple text messages among widely dispersed computers did exist at that time, they were primitive and their usage was largely confined to computer scientists and specialists.

Dr. Michelson challenged me to create an electronic version of the interoffice, inter-organizational paper mail system in use at UMDNJ at the time. For reasons that will become clear later, I want to emphasize that I was not asked to make a simple "electronic messaging system" or a "text messaging system." I was asked **to create the electronic equivalent of the entire interoffice mail system and all its features --- to create email, the system we all know and experience today.**

I began with an evaluation of UMDNJ's paper-based mail system, the same system that was used in offices around the world. This challenge to digitize the paper based mail system became my passion and mission. I worked in the

Lab nearly every day and also at home on our kitchen table, often until 2AM.

Overall, I wrote nearly 50,000 lines of code across a system of 35 programs to design and implement an electronic version of that mail system, and I named it "email," a term never before recognized in the English language.

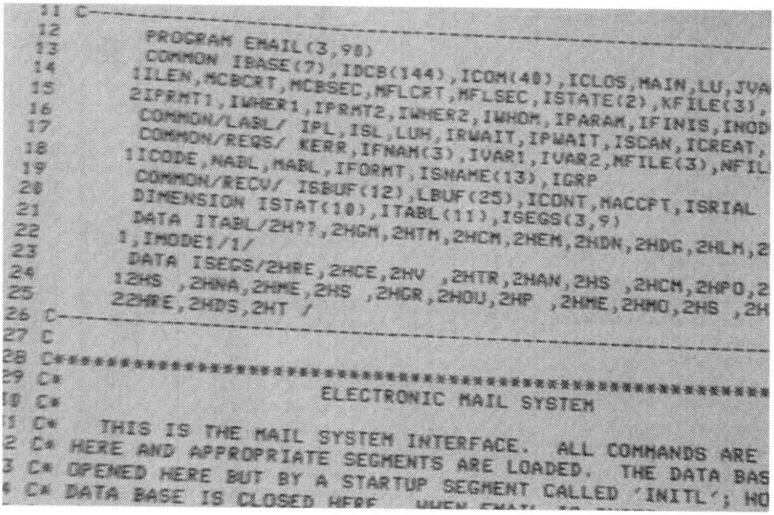

```
11 C-----------------------------------------------------------------
12
13       PROGRAM EMAIL(3,98)
14       COMMON IBASE(7),IDCB(144),ICOM(40),ICLOS,MAIN,LU,JVA
15      1ILEN,MCBCRT,MCBSEC,MFLCRT,MFLSEC,ISTATE(2),KFILE(3),
16      2IPRMT1,IWHER1,IPRMT2,IWHER2,IWHOM,IPARAM,IFINIS,INOD
17       COMMON/LABL/ IPL,ISL,LUH,IRWAIT,IPWAIT,ISCAN,ICREAT,
18       COMMON/REQS/ KERR,IFNAM(3),IVAR1,IVAR2,MFILE(3),NFIL
19      1ICODE,NABL,MABL,IFORMT,ISNAME(13),IGRP
20       COMMON/RECV/ ISBUF(12),LBUF(25),ICONT,MACCPT,ISRIAL
21       DIMENSION ISTAT(10),ITABL(11),ISEGS(3,9)
22       DATA ITABL/2H??,2HGM,2HTM,2HCM,2HEM,2HDN,2HDG,2HLM,2
23      1,IMODE1/1/
24       DATA ISEGS/2HRE,2HCE,2HV ,2HTR,2HAN,2HS ,2HCM,2HPO,2
25      12HS ,2HNA,2HME,2HS ,2HGR,2HOU,2HP ,2HME,2HMO,2HS ,2H
26      22HRE,2HDS,2HT /
26 C-----------------------------------------------------------------
27 C
28 C****************************************************************
29 C*
30 C*                      ELECTRONIC MAIL SYSTEM
31 C*     THIS IS THE MAIL SYSTEM INTERFACE.  ALL COMMANDS ARE
32 C* HERE AND APPROPRIATE SEGMENTS ARE LOADED.  THE DATA BAS
33 C* OPENED HERE BUT BY A STARTUP SEGMENT CALLED 'INITL'; HO
34 C* DATA BASE IS CLOSED HERE
```

Chapter Nine

What It Was and Why

But what was email, exactly? As I originally conceived it, and as it still is today, email is a *system* designed to be the electronic replica of the many features and functions of the time-honored interoffice mail system that used paper documents to enable collaboration, cooperation and communication among users of differing expertise within the business office environment.

The interoffice mail system consisted of multiple and interlocked systems including the following:

- The secretary's physical desktop with a typewriter, inbox and outbox, pens and pencils, paper clips, and other useful implements.

- Interoffice mail memo and envelopes with spaces to indicate "to," "from," "subject," and "date."
- Multiple options for sending and processing such as pneumatic tubes, hand delivery in the office, or courier to outlying locations.

Looking back on this whole experience, I want to emphasize a few facts that are important for their own sake, and also because they contrast with some conventional ideas about innovation.

First, the work took place off the beaten track in a small computer lab in Newark, New Jersey. It wasn't funded by the government or the military or a large corporation.

Second, it was motivated not by potential profit, but simply as a way to help people -- mostly women -- who worked in the offices at UMDNJ.

These people were not a "target audience" or a "target market" or a "demographic" that we were marketing to for making billions. They were my friends. Success would be measured not by how much money was made, but by how much their lives were made easier. With this is mind, the program had to be easy for anyone to use.

At that time there was a belief that using a computer had to be difficult and highly technical. It was and would have to remain in the realm of a trained academic elite and "nerds." Of course, underlying this was the conviction that ordinary people were simply too stupid to use computers.

A final point: there was not the slightest degree of secrecy about the project. People were always coming and going in our lab, including other researchers, local community people, IT folks, and vendors such as from Hewlett-Packard and IBM. We printed and shared our manuals with others. There were no non-disclosure agreements, and I even held seminars about the project. We were not Apple or Google, not showing our developments to others, and shielding it in the utmost secrecy. In summary, we were fully transparent. Over the years, thousands had direct contact with my invention.

It was happening in the same improvised spirit as Steve Wozniak's Homebrew Computer Club, which was the forerunner of Apple. This was done in Newark by people who loved science. It could have happened anywhere, just as many great innovations have originated in obscure locations. That has always been true and it always will be, despite the efforts of large corporations, the military and academic elite to tell us otherwise.

West Essex Tribune October 30, 1980

Shiva Ayyadurai shows plans for the electronic mail system that he designed to math teacher Irman Greenberg and Stella Oleksiak, coordinator of the Independent Study program at Livingston High School.

Livingston Student Designs Electronic Mail System

On October 7, Irman Greenberg, math teacher, and Stella Oleksiak, Independent Study coordinator, along with Shiva Ayyadurai and his father visited the Computer Center at the College of Medicine and

learned various computer languages such as Fortran, Basic, Cobol and Snobol, and was graduated with honors. As a consequence of his math background and his computer training, he began his work at

Chapter Ten

Coming to MIT

I was very happy with the way my work in Dr. Michelson's lab at UMDNJ turned out. It was a grand success. Hundreds used the application, and I had made people's lives easier. Just as we had planned, it was a computer program that was the electronic equivalent of the paper-based interoffice mail. It was email, and nothing like this comprehensive system had been done before. But once it was done, this innovation did not dominate my life. Trying to profit from it or market it in any way never occurred to me.

I continued my commitment to doing well in school, and won nearly every award that the school had to give.

Then something unexpected happened. It was one of those turning points that seems to come out of nowhere, but when you look back it's impossible to imagine what would have happened without it.

My mother was at a mall, where she happened to meet two women from India who did not have a place to stay. She invited the women to our house, and we got to know them. One of them had left her husband because she had fallen in love with another man.

As it happened, I myself had fallen in love with Lorraine Monetti, the proverbial "girl next door." It was a pleasure to go over to Lorraine's house and see the way her parents, Teddy and Gloria, seemed like two love birds. But Teddy was also a man's man. He took me to baseball and soccer games. Together we saw the great Pele's last game in the Meadowlands.

Sometimes my mom felt I was wasting my time socializing with Lorraine and her father, but my mother was much more flexible regarding the Indian woman from the mall who had left her husband for another man. That man's name was Gopal, and he also visited our home.

Gopal was the first person to tell me about MIT. Before that I had never heard of the place. He told me that it was the number one science and technology institute in the world. In retrospect, I wonder why my guidance counselor had never told me about MIT. The counselor at the time was encouraging me to apply to one of the local state schools: Stevens Institute of Technology. I was either number 1 or 2 in the entire class of nearly 600 students, and LHS was one of the best public schools in the country.

Gopal, however, was insistent that I absolutely must go to MIT, and he showed me a brochure, which I still clearly remember with the words: "Massachusetts Institute of Technology."

Although the picture of the domed building on the MIT brochure was impressive, I was not interested in applying. An "Institute" was a definitely a turnoff word. It seemed to lack any collegiate spirit.

But Gopal would not give up. He didn't leave me alone until I filled out the application. Strangely, the application asked for a hand drawing of my favorite cartoon character: I drew "Beetle Bailey," from a comic strip about a bumbling soldier. They must have liked that character, because I was accepted.

My first visit to the MIT campus was not encouraging. I went with my mother, and the first student we saw looked old, unhealthy, and unhappy, all hunched over and carrying a big knapsack. I was still determined not to attend MIT. It seemed very big and very unfriendly.

Massachusetts Institute of Technology

TECH TALK

September 2, 1981
Volume 26
Number 5

The Class of 1985 arrives to meet the Institute

By JOANNE MILLER
Staff Writer

They are accomplished in a variety of other ways as well. One designed an electronic mail system now being used at the New Jersey College of Medicine and Dentistry; another designed and built solar panels now in use at

But my high school AP physics instructor Mrs. Samuels encouraged me to go, and said that I would love Boston --- the "Athens" of the world. I had a lot of respect for her. She had survived the Holocaust and had a number tattooed on her arm. Her son was doing his PhD at MIT and loved it.

I decided to go, but reluctantly. Maybe it was my dharma, my destiny. It was certainly an important part of my life's journey.

I arrived at the campus on September 2, 1981 and my email invention was highlighted on the front page of MIT's official newspaper, with two other students' work. I didn't think that much of it, but it was an honor that the invention of email was featured among those two other students of the entering class of 1,041 new students.

My life at time of entering MIT was both typically collegiate and decidedly unconventional. I had enough Advanced

Placement credits to graduate MIT in two years if I wanted. However, I was interested in other things --- larger scale systems --- motivated by my interest in the caste system I experienced in India and also wanting to understand how a woman, my grandmother, with no degrees was able to heal people through the system of India's traditional medicine, Siddha.

Chapter Eleven

Inventor of Email

When I was elected freshman class president, this earned me a dinner meeting at the home of the president of MIT, Paul E. Gray. It turned out to be an important and enlightening meeting that began to open my eyes to the business and political aspects of innovation.

Dr. Gray told me it was "unfortunate that Supreme Court didn't recognize software patents," and it was he who urged me to apply for a Copyright to protect my invention of email. He saw the "money side" of innovation. Nothing like this had ever occurred to me.

At the time of my inventing email in 1978, neither Copyright law nor patent law was in place for protecting software inventions.

In 1980, the United States government passed the Computer Software Act of 1980, which amended the Copyright Act of 1976, to protect software inventions through Copyright. The lawmakers in Washington thought that software was like sheet music --- just written work.

On August 30, 1982, the United States government issued the first U.S. Copyright for "Email," to Shiva Ayyadurai, legally recognizing me as the inventor of email.

Three important and indisputable facts, therefore, stand without question concerning why I am the inventor of email: (1) I was the first to create a full-scale electronic replica of the interoffice mail system; (2) I was the first to name this system "email,"; and (3) I received that first U.S. Copyright for "Email."

CERTIFICATE OF COPYRIGHT REGISTRATION

This certificate, issued under the seal of the Copyright Office in accordance with the provisions of section 410(a) of title 17, United States Code, attests that copyright registration has been made for the work identified below. The information in this certificate has been made a part of the Copyright Office records.

REGISTER OF COPYRIGHTS
United States of America

FORM TX
UNITED STATES COPYRIGHT OFFICE

REGISTRATION NUMBER
TXu 111-775

TX TXU

EFFECTIVE DATE OF REGISTRATION
8 30 82
Month Day Year

DO NOT WRITE ABOVE THIS LINE. IF YOU NEED MORE SPACE, USE A SEPARATE CONTINUATION SHEET.

1 TITLE OF THIS WORK ▼
EMAIL

PREVIOUS OR ALTERNATIVE TITLES ▼
Computer program for Electronic Mail System

PUBLICATION AS A CONTRIBUTION If this work was published as a contribution to a periodical, serial, or collection, give information about the collective work in which the contribution appeared. Title of Collective Work ▼

If published in a periodical or serial give: Volume ▼ Number ▼ Issue Date ▼ On Pages ▼

2 a NAME OF AUTHOR ▼
Mr. Shiva Ayyadurai

DATES OF BIRTH AND DEATH
Year Born ▼ 1963 Year Died ▼

Was this contribution to the work a "work made for hire"? ☐ Yes ☐ No

AUTHOR'S NATIONALITY OR DOMICILE
Name of Country
OR Citizen of ▶
Domiciled in ▶ United States

WAS THIS AUTHOR'S CONTRIBUTION TO THE WORK
Anonymous? ☐ Yes ☒ No
Pseudonymous? ☐ Yes ☒ No
If the answer to either of these questions is "Yes," see detailed instructions.

NOTE
Under the law, the "author" of a

NATURE OF AUTHORSHIP Briefly describe nature of the material created by this author in which copyright is claimed. ▼
Created and Write entire text of the computer program.

It was not until 1994 that the United States Court of Appeals for the Federal Circuit ruled that computer programs were patentable as the equivalent of a "digital machine." Up until then, Copyright was the only way to protect software inventions. And, it was a non-trivial process to get such a Copyright. I had to fill out a complicated form, print, organize, and send thousands of lines of program code in specific format. I did all of this as a teenager, without any attorney.

Therefore, my being issued the first Copyright for email in 1982 is of immense historical and legal significance. It was not just a matter of putting the "©" symbol as we do today. At that time, Copyrighting of software, and disclosing it was a significant event. One of the world's leading Intellectual Property (IP) attorneys, Stephen Y. Chow has made this eminently clear in his legal opinion:

"In August 1982, the U.S. Copyright Office of the Library of Congress registered Shiva Ayyadurai's email code and user's manual. According to its records these were the first works registered under the title, 'Email,' preceding the next such registration by two years. Dr. Ayyadurai's registrations and deposits showed to the world his reduction to practice of his email system.

These registrations were remarkable for an eighteen-year old student, involving non-trivial procedures under a Copyright Act only recently open to protecting software. Protecting software creations by copyright was the common wisdom of the day. Not only were patents largely disfavored during decades preceding the creation in 1982 of the Federal Circuit Court of Appeals, the Supreme Court had held software unpatentable unless it was adjunct to a physical process. Only in 1994 did the Federal Circuit recognize software as patentable for creating new physical machines in conjunction with the computers the software programmed (recently the Supreme Court limited this principle).

Had the patenting path for software been considered possible in 1982 generally and particularly by the MIT community, I have little doubt that Dr. Ayyadurai would have pursued it. In fact, unlike later software copyright owners who kept their code secret and deposited only identifying portions, Dr. Ayyadurai kept with the original reading of the United States Constitution provision for patents and copyrights to promote disclosure in return for limited exclusivity. Unlike many, in return for protection of his code, Dr. Ayyadurai contributed to the public the ideas shown and searchable in his 'Email' deposits in the Library of Congress."

Part Three

Fight for the American Dream

Chapter Twelve

What I Really Learned at MIT

As I continued at MIT, I gained a level of political information and sophistication that I never expected to find at MIT.

Through the Student Government, I met Arnold Contreras, a Mexican-American, a "Chicano" from Texas. I liked his fighting spirit in demanding student government leaders be more fair in how they disbursed funds. He and I became friends. Around the same time I left the fraternity. I didn't see much "brotherhood" there.

I met Jespal Singh while I was playing Varsity Soccer. He schooled me in Marxism-Leninism. Jespal was a Harvard Grad student, a

Sikh, and he had a deep political analysis. He saw Nehru and Gandhi as men who sold out the Indian people. Through Jespal I met other Marxist Leninists in Boston. He also gave me a very important book: *The Rise and Fall of the East India Company*.

Another responsibility of being president of the freshman class was membership on the class Ring Committee. Here, I saw ring vendors "bribing" student government officers with expensive dinners. In fact, every Ring Committee member was supposed to get a free ring. The Ring Committee was responsible for choosing a vendor on behalf of the entire Class. If Ring Committee members were getting free rings, would they not select the vendor that had the most expensive ring?

I exposed this corruption and resigned from the Ring Committee. It seemed as though the MIT extracurricular system was teaching student

GA chooses Ayyadurai

By Tony Zamparutti

The Undergraduate Association General Assembly (GA) elected Shiva Ayyadurai '85 its new floor leader at Thursday's GA meeting.

Former GA floor leader James Taylor '84, a member of the faculty Committee on Educational Policy (CEP), told the General Assembly the CEP is reconsidering its proposal to change freshman pass/no credit. Faculty members questioned the premises and the provisions of the CEP plan at last Wednesday's faculty meeting.

About thirty GA representatives attended the meeting, including one student carrying a portable television set. Before the meeting, Undergraduate Association (UA) President Kenneth Segel '83 and Secretary General Katherine Adams '84 served strawberry and banana daiquiris.

The General Assembly also tabled a motion, proposed by Ayyadurai, requiring that members of class ring committees not accept free rings from the manufacturer. Kenneth Freedman '84, who ran against Ayyadurai for GA floor leader, was the chief opponent of the motion.

(Please turn to page 7)

Through experience in student government, Ayyadurai said, "I have been fortunate in acquiring some sense of why student government may seem ineffective."

"The role of a GA rep. must take on a new dimension — that of initiator," Ayyadurai told the members. "We . . . must seek issues of importance within our constituency and bring those issues to the limelight."

Freedman, in his candidacy speech for GA floor leader, told the assembly, "I feel I can help revamp the GA." He said he would restructure GA committees, increase publicity of UA elections, urge representatives to attend GA meetings, and find a guest speaker for each meeting.

Although the GA floor leader can have a lot of influence, former floor leader James Taylor '84 said, "The only thing you have to do is make sure the minutes are out and the agenda is typed."

The General Assembly tabled Ayyadurai's motion setting specific bylaws for all class ring committees after a long and inconclusive debate. Freedman and Class of 1985 President Robin Barker opposed Ayyadurai's proposal.

leaders at early age, the "pay for play" model --- a.k.a. Corruption.

I was also elected president of Sangam, the Indian student's organization. It was filled with Brahmins, directly from India who had not had the American experience. They were on a narrow track to get a degree, get married, and perpetuate Indian feudalism. I left that organization too as I saw them have little to no interest in discussing politics or addressing the inequities of Indian culture. They seemed to just want to throw Diwali parties, get drunk and find their suitable mate.

I was interested in understanding why the Indian caste system existed. I studied the origins of the Indian caste system with the world-renowned Professor Noam Chomsky. Around this time, when Dean Hope -- the first black dean at MIT -- was fired, I started *The Student*, a radical newspaper. By my senior year I was thoroughly radicalized and revolutionized. I took part in

1986 Burning the South African Flag in Show of Solidarity to End Apartheid

massive demonstrations to save Dean Hope's job and against Reagan's war in El Salvador.

I was active and led many protests for ensuring more woman, poor students --- black and white, and minorities could attend MIT. I organized anti-apartheid and divestment movement protests to force MIT to withdraw its investments in racist South Africa, and burned the South African flag on the MIT Student Center steps in defiance.

When a fellow MIT student, during his trip back home to Sri Lanka, was jailed by the genocidal Sri Lankan government, which was killing indigenous Tamils, I led a major march on the home of the MIT President, who had invited Sri Lanka's President during that time.

At MIT, I learned how to organize, and integrate political history into day-to-day activism on campus. MIT didn't really train me in science during my undergraduate days, but provided me the stage to learn how to how to fight. Because of these "extra-curricular" activities, I sacrificed my accelerated career path, which I had originally been on upon entering MIT, by not graduating until 1986.

Chapter Thirteen

Beyond Email

In the years immediately after my graduation, the Internet changed the world. In 1993, when the World Wide Web (WWW) became available, the Internet became accessible to the every day consumer. Email use exploded and a true electronic communications revolution was unleashed, such as the world had never seen before.

Until then, the use of email had been mostly confined to business or the government. But with the introduction of the WWW, everybody could send emails to anybody they wanted. And that's exactly what everybody did.

Before 1993, email was strictly a business application. But then, suddenly, everybody was sending email messages. For political leaders, it was not a good idea to ignore those attempted communications. No matter how inconsequential they might seem, writing to the President was an important experience for a farmer sitting at a kitchen table or a student in a college library.

The Clinton White House had twenty interns who were sorting 5000 emails a day into 147 patterned categories including education, drugs, and many more.

In an attempt to bring this situation under control, the government announced a competition for analyzing and sorting the emails. No such thing had ever been done before, because there had been no need for anything like this. I entered the competition and won.

The Christian Science Monitor

CHEERING ON THE INGENUITY OF TODAY'S AND TOMORROW'S INNOVATORS

By Kirsten A. Conover | MARCH 12, 1996

This year's Lemelson-MIT Prize-winner and Student Prize-winner will be announced April 11 and May 1, respectively.

Student inventors, in particular, represent an untapped resource of creative and entrepreneurial energy, according to benefactor Jerome Lemelson, who is responsible for the touch-controlled cassette-tape drive (found in the

Shiva Ayyadurai, founder of Millennium Productions, and inventor of the White House Encryption System. When President Clinton needed a reliable encryption system for his electronic mail, he turned to Mr. Ayyadurai, whose classification system beat those of industry leaders.

Now he is hosting a virtual-reality art show titled "Crossing Lines": billed as the first international internet multimedia arts exhibit on racism and discrimination - with the goal of bringing art and technology together. (Its Internet address is: http://www.arts-online.com/ crossinglines.html). He and his staff also design home pages for arts organizations such as the Alvin Ailey Dance Company and the Handel & Haydn Society.

Before long, as I looked at thousands of emails a day, I had an important realization: they were not all that different. In fact, looking below the surface of the contents, the emails were almost robotically repetitious. I had done extensive academic work on pattern recognition, including the classification of people's handwriting. Now I was starting to recognize patterns of content in those thousands of emails. I suspected that content could be organized around a certain number of thoughts and ideas just as I'd organized the physical properties of handwriting.

I created some algorithms to detect an email's essential features. I named the software Xiva, and founded a company called Information Cybernetics to market the idea. That was in 1994, when major retailers were starting to make full-scale commitments to the Internet, including email and online marketing. Jeff Bezos would introduce Amazon.com in July of the following year.

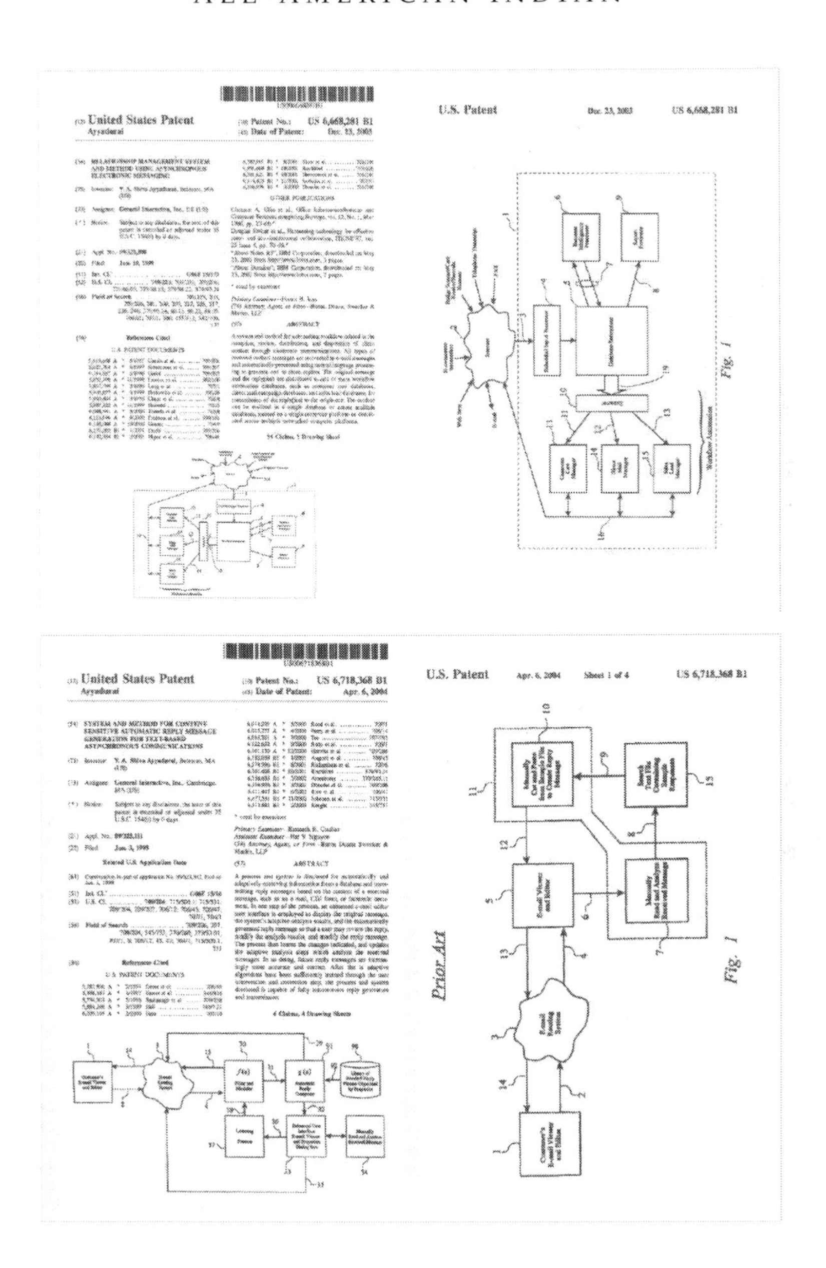

United States Patent
Ayyadurai

Patent No.: US 6,668,281 B1
Date of Patent: Dec. 23, 2003

U.S. Patent Dec. 23, 2003 US 6,668,281 B1

Fig. 1

United States Patent
Ayyadurai

Patent No.: US 6,718,368 B1
Date of Patent: Apr. 6, 2004

SYSTEM AND METHOD FOR CONTENT SENSITIVE AUTOMATIC REPLY MESSAGE GENERATION FOR TEXT-BASED ASYNCHRONOUS COMMUNICATIONS

ABSTRACT

4 Claims, 4 Drawing Sheets

U.S. Patent Apr. 6, 2004 Sheet 1 of 4 US 6,718,368 B1

Prior Art

Fig. 1

When I learned that AT&T needed help with its surprising volume of email, I sought an introduction. No matter how Web commerce unfolded, I saw that big firms would get lots of online messages and would have to deal with them. After a pilot demonstration of Xiva – which I trademarked as EchoMail -- AT&T signed on in 1996.

The basis for classifying and decoding email was surprisingly simple: human communication is not as diverse as we think it is. EchoMail scans emails for keywords and phrases that characterize the few fundamental properties that are of interest to a company in any email.

For example, is the email about a billing problem, or a merchandise return, or a legal problem? EchoMail evaluates an email and sorts it in the correct category. The program does this by applying a dictionary of key words and word relationships known as a semantic network. If the program finds the word 'website' and 'problem'

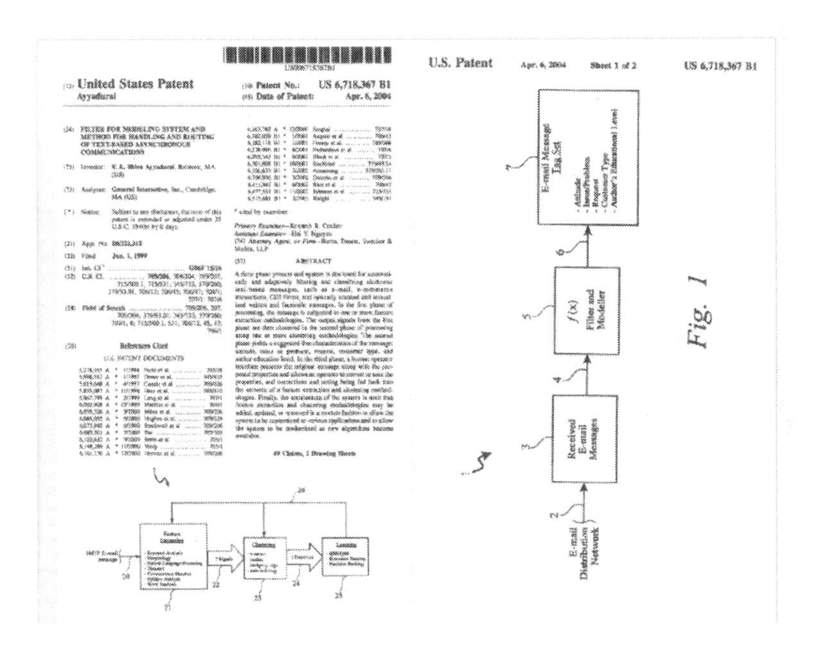

United States Patent
Ayyadurai

Patent No.: US 6,718,367 B1
Date of Patent: Apr. 6, 2004

ABSTRACT

U.S. Patent Apr. 6, 2004 Sheet 1 of 2 US 6,718,367 B1

close to one another, it might conclude that the email's issue is an online ordering problem. Depending on how an email is classified, EchoMail can choose either to reply from a selection of pre written responses, or forward the message to one or more departments for humans to address.

EchoMail could also classify the email as negative, neutral, or positive by homing in on keywords such as "terrible" or "superb." One message included the words "da bomb." EchoMail initially classified this as negative, but when we learned 'da bomb' means 'you're cool' we changed the classification. Finally, EchoMail could benefit marketing by classifying customer types. Email writers often give away such information as whether they own a boat, or their home address and zip code. EchoMail can add this information to the client's customer databases.

Subsequently I began work on CytoSolve, a technology platform for eliminating animal testing and accelerating drug development. To date, CytoSolve has been used to discover a new combination therapeutic for pancreatic cancer, gaining FDA allowance to proceed to clinical trials in a record 11 months. CytoSolve has also been used to demonstrate the lack of safety standards of genetically engineered foods (GMOs).

Chapter Fourteen

The "Big Fight" Begins

Based on my work on CytoSolve, MIT awarded me a PhD. In 2007 I received a Fulbright Grant to return to India to study the traditional Indian health systems of Siddha, which is taught primarily in South India, and Ayurveda, which is taught in the North, from a systems biology perspective. I discovered that the Siddhars, the healers, had always been systems thinkers. Unlike conventional Western medicine, they were not reductionist. They didn't look at people and their health in a fragmented way. Their view of health was genuinely holistic.

I discovered shared concepts and categories that linked Siddha with modern control systems theory. This was a major breakthrough, and would become the basis of my future teaching.

While in India, in June of 2009, I was recruited for an eminent position in the Indian scientific establishment. I was appointed head of Innovation in the largest science institution in all of India, serving 1.2 billion people. Suddenly I was being treated like a raja, with a beautiful home, servants, car, invited to state dinners. My position was Additional Secretary in the Indian Government, equivalent to a Deputy Director in the US Cabinet. I was the Golden Boy.

I never asked for this position. I was in India on a Fulbright Scholarship to study Siddha as a MIT-trained systems biologist. But the Director General of the powerful Council of Scientific and Industrial Research (CSIR), Samir Brahmachari, had my dossier.

Volume 52 – Number 2
Wednesday, September 19, 2007

TechTalk
SERVING THE MIT COMMUNITY

Fulbright scholar in new adventure

Anne Trafton
News Office

In the 26 years since he first arrived at MIT as a freshman, V.A. Shiva Ayyadurai has earned four MIT degrees and started two multimillion-dollar companies.

This fall, he will use his most recent degree, a Ph.D. in computational systems biology, and a Fulbright Scholarship to explore one of his lifelong interests: the intersection of Eastern and Western medicine.

Ayyadurai's upcoming project is the latest in a series of personal ventures that have spanned fields as diverse as electronic communications, animation and molecular biology. His experience shows what is possible with an MIT education, he says.

"I don't think I could have done this anywhere else," said Ayyadurai, 43. "MIT is a great place to follow your dreams."

Ayyadurai started dreaming as a child in India, where his grandfather was a farmer and his grandmother a shaman, or traditional healer. He became interested in medicine watching his grandmother diagnose and treat patients based on a system of "elements"—earth, water, fire, metal and wood. That approach may seem strange to Westerners, but "you'd see people actually getting healed," he said.

When Ayyadurai started as a freshman at MIT in 1981, he planned to go to medical school but later changed his plans. He found Western medicine, with its dependence on looking up symptoms in reference books, very different from his grandmother's practice. "There was always something sterile about Western medicine," he said. "I got turned off by it."

Now, he wants to explore what Eastern and Western medical traditions can learn from each other. Ayyadurai sees the exchange as a two-way street. He plans to apply Western scientific rigor to testing the long-established traditions of the East, and to study how the Eastern "elements" can inform Western medicine.

He points out that the market for alternative therapies based on Eastern medicine is growing every year, even without scientific evidence to support their usefulness.

"Let's look at glucosamine and see if it really works. Let's look at ginkgo and see if it really works," he said.

Ayyadurai departs for India this month to begin his studies, and he also plans to start raising funds to launch an MIT-affiliated center to study Eastern medicine.

Road to success

Ayyadurai's path to the Fulbright Scholarship has been marked by early and frequent successes in a variety of fields.

He moved to New Jersey with his par-

See FULBRIGHT
Page 3

PHOTO / DONNA COVENEY

Shiva Ayyadurai, Ph.D., won a Fulbright scholarship to travel to India and study Eastern medicine.

Brain's messengers could be regulated

MIT researchers find potential for better understanding of schizophrenia

Deborah Halber
News Office Correspondent

Researchers at MIT's Picower Institute for Learning and Memory have found that tiny, spontaneous releases of the brain's primary chemical messengers can be regulated, potentially giving scientists unprecedented control over how the brain is wired.

The work, reported in the Sept. 16 early online edition of Nature Neuroscience, could lead to a better understanding of neurological diseases like schizophrenia.

Sputtering electrical activity—like a firecracker's leftover sparks after a big bang—was long considered inconsequential background noise compared with the main cell-to-cell interactions underlying thought and memory.

But lead author J. Troy Littleton, Fred and Carole Middleton Associate Professor of Biology at MIT, and colleagues found that the minuscule events that follow a burst of electrical and chemical activity among neurons are far more important that previously thought. A breakdown in this molecular mechanism could be the culprit in schizophrenia and other neurological diseases, the authors reported.

Neurons communicate with one another through chemical junctions called synapses. Key to the system are complexins. These small proteins play a role in the release of the brain's chemical messen-

See BRAIN
Page 4

Mr. Brahmachari knew everything about me: four degrees from MIT, publications, and the fact listed in some documents that I was the boy who invented email in 1978.

And when I took the job I thought it was a dream come true. I could work from within the system to serve the Indian masses through science. As a young boy, I had made a promise to my grandparents, that I would one day return to do something exactly like this.

All my life, science and invention were all I ate, slept, and breathed. But what really moved and intrigued me was the system of human oppression and how to solve that. For I had experienced that first hand in my life and in my family's life as a "low caste" Hindu.

I never wanted to come to MIT. But when I came, it set me on a path to become a systems revolutionary of sorts. I had fought MIT, on many issues. But now, in India, I thought I could focus on my science, and contribute to the fields of health, as well as eastern and western systems of medicine.

This was when disaster struck, and it went on striking for quite some time.

I got word that the report I had published had upset some powerful people. Indian bureaucrats don't like their dirty laundry being shared with the public. I had also given a television interview, prime time, that was broadcast all over India. Incredible as it seemed, I was advised to flee the country immediately. If I didn’t, I would be arrested and jailed. After that there was no telling what would happen.

I grabbed my passport and wallet, which had about 10,000 Rupees and we left. Reela, the woman to whom I was married at that time, took my cell phone and I took hers. Her father had told us, we were being tracked. I jumped on a train going North, up to the Himalayas and the Nepal border.

The goal was to cross that border quietly. John Bradley, my long-time attorney and ex-military man with connections to US intelligence agencies, advised me on how to get out of India, without being detected.

This was how I found myself on a 32-hour train ride across northern India from New Delhi to the border with Nepal. Uncomfortable though it was, I had plenty time to think about where I was, where I was coming from, and where I was going.

I was escaping the country. I had been threatened with arrest because I'd done a television interview about my work with India's Council of Scientific and Industrial Research (C.S.I.R.) a government-funded agency plagued by corruption and bureaucratic inefficiency.

The US embassy had advised me not to do the interview. I was even requested to come to the embassy for protection. Instead I did the interview with India's largest television news network and it ran for eight minutes in prime time. So now I was on the train.

Looking around at my fellow passengers, I recognized the "real" people of India. Farmers, tradesmen, families, the old and the young. Perhaps, scattered among them, were others escaping just like me. Yes, I was aware of differences between myself and these people. But in my heart I didn't feel different at all.

By conventional measures, I qualified as a member of the elite. I had been recruited by the Indian government for that key position with C.S.I.R. I had four degrees from the Massachusetts Institute of Technology, including a PhD in biological engineering.

But none of that mattered compared to the connection I felt with those people on the train. I was a dark-skinned, lower caste Indian. My grandmother was a healer in a rural village, using the arts of traditional Indian medicine. Although my family had moved to the United States when I was in grade school, we lived in Newark, New Jersey, another marginalized outback. I always felt connected to India, and I went back every year.

The government bureaucracy of India was stealing from these people. It wasn't their money that was stolen -- they didn't have any money – it was any hope or opportunity they might have for positive change. The C.S.I.R. organization was supposed to nurture creativity and innovation for the future of the country. Instead, its hypocrisy and corruption insured that things would stay exactly the same, or get worse.

I couldn't back away from giving that television interview. I couldn't settle into my government-provided house like a good and grateful little boy. My grandmother had told me too many folk tales of heroic warrior gods and goddesses. That's why I found myself on the train.

Yes, I was escaping, but it was only a tactical retreat in order to open new battlefronts elsewhere.

I was in a fire storm. I was put in a position to lead and protect these 4500 scientists on behalf of India's vast population.

Today, looking back on that train ride -- as well as my fighting as an activist scientist, in both America and in India -- I see how I was being trained for the even more intense struggle I would face when I got back to America.

Chapter Fifteen

"The Big Fight" Continues

When I returned to Boston, my mother was dying of pulmonary fibrosis. Much to my surprise, she presented me with a suitcase filled with all the artifacts of my early work on email -- my fifty thousand lines of code, everything.

One of my colleagues, a professor at Emerson College reviewed the materials and contacted Doug Aamoth, the technology editor at Time magazine. He went through all my material. In fact he was the only journalist who ever actually did so, including journals who were aggressively critical of me. Doug Aamoth wrote a feature article entitled "The Man Who Invented Email," which informed the general public about email's true origin.

In 2012, the Smithsonian Institution's National Museum of American History requested and received the artifacts that documented my work, which really did epitomize the American Dream.

An event was held at the Smithsonian to celebrate the acquisition of all that material. The stated purpose of the museum's acquisition of my material, and the plan to display it, was to inspire young people to become innovators. This was completely initiated by the Smithsonian. It was an honor, but I did not stand to benefit in any tangible way, and certainly not financially.

When my papers were received by the Smithsonian's National Museum of American History on February 16, 2012, a *Washington Post* reporter wrote an article entitled, "V.A. Shiva

TIME MAGAZINE SUBSCRIBE PHOTOS VIDEOS LISTS APPS LIFE

TIME The Man Who Invented Email

By DOUG AAMOTH

PHOTO BY DONNA COVENEY

Ayyadurai: Inventor of Email Honored by the Smithsonian."

This article and the facts it stated perturbed a multibillion-dollar marketing myth perpetrated by the Raytheon Corporation, one of the largest defense contractors in America. This myth contends, among other things, that inserting the "@" sign between the username and the host server is equivalent to inventing email. The @ sign innovation was developed by the late Ray Tomlinson, a Raytheon employee.

The Raytheon Corporation competes in a robust and expanding $70 billion cybersecurity market. In 2014, Raytheon won $260 million in cybersecurity business and cited "reputation" among "principal competitive factors" considered by customers. Ray Tomlinson is touted as "the inventor of email" to establish this "reputation," and acquire new cybersecurity clients.

Raytheon and its cabal of supporters used the occasion of my gaining legitimate recognition for the invention of email in order to discredit me. They attacked the *Washington Post* reporter and forced her editors to print a completely nebulous correction that I "was not the inventor of electronic messaging." Of course, I never claimed to be the inventor of electronic messaging, whose history goes back to the Morse Code telegraph of the 1800s.

Part of this cabal was a group called Special Interest Group for Computers, Information and Society (SIGCIS.) Its chief spokesperson, Thomas Haigh, has attacked me in a purported "scholarly" blog while thanking contributors from Raytheon and others, all of whom have vested interests in perpetuating their own lies.

After three decades of not promoting my work, these people attacked me as if I were a money-hungry opportunist. The online gossip site Gizmodo called me an "asshole," "a dick," and "a fraud." There were threats that "the curry-stained Indian should be shot and hanged by his dhothi."

Chapter Sixteen

Defending the American Dream

Email is not the simple exchange of text messages, or "electronic messaging." Email is not the Morse code telegraph of the mid 1800s; or the 1939 IBM radio-type; or messaging through ARPANET, a precursor to today's internet; or even the familiar "@" sign, which was used in early electronic communications.

I have never claimed to have invented electronic messaging or the @ sign. I invented email, the electronic replica or duplication of the paper-based interoffice mail system.

The significance of my copyright of the word "email" has also been challenged. But this copyright was extremely significant. It was the only form of legal protection for software available at the time -- and I was urged to copyright "email" by the president of MIT, hardly someone who wasted time on anything insignificant.

It's important to understand that, in 1978, electronic messaging researchers and so-called "internet pioneers" considered it impossible to create something like email. In December of 1977, a few months before I invented email, an "internet pioneer" named David Crocker clearly stated this in the introduction to a seminal RAND Corporation Report. This summarized the state-of-the-art research in electronic messaging at the time:

> *"At this time [December, 1977], no attempt is being made to emulate the full-scale, inter-organizational mail system. To construct a fully-detailed and monolithic message processing*

> *environment requires a much larger effort than has been possible. [p.4]*
>
> *In addition, the fact that the system is intended for use in various organizational contexts and by users of differing expertise makes it almost impossible to build a system which responds to all users' needs. Consequently, important segments of a full message environment have received little or no attention [p.7].*

In 1978 I did not think it "impossible" to create a full-scale electronic replica of the inter-organizational paper-based mail system. If I had thought so, I never would have done it. But I did do it.

It is worth noting, and it is also reprehensible, that more than 35 years after email's invention David Crocker is still leading a campaign to defame email's inventor. Perhaps this is in order to make the world forget his own December 1977 statements, and to revise history to the effect that email was created as a "collaboration" of ARPANET and "internet pioneers."

As the factual record shows, the ARPANET information brochure of 1978, and even the one of 1986 (eight years later) makes no reference to the word "email," "e-mail" or "Electronic Mail" either in the body of the brochure or in the index of their brochure. What is fraudulent is to claim now that the "ARPANET invented email."

Why were there such vicious attacks against me? The reason is simple. The idea that a 14 year old immigrant boy working in an obscure hospital could invent email disrupted the carefully nurtured storyline that major innovations always had to come from the triangle of big corporations, major universities and the military --- what President Eisenhower and

Senator Fulbright had referred to as the "military-industrial-academic" complex.

Major innovations had to come from defense contractors. When they did, defense contractors could receive whatever huge funding they wanted, because so many wonderful things like email came out of that -- which in actuality had not come from military initiatives.

But the facts on who invented email are black and white. There never was a genuine controversy. This whole media storm was fabricated to continue brainwashing Americans with the idea that innovations come from war. The attacks on my reputation were libelous and defamatory. However, I was not able to find an attorney to take on this Goliath of an enemy.

Finally, in 2016, after years of attempting to find legal representation, I signed with Charles Harder, the attorney who represented the ex-pro wrestler "Hulk Hogan" in a highly publicized case against Gawker Media. Charles Harder filed a suit against Gawker Media and I was victorious on November 1, 2016 when Gawker Media settled with me for $750,000, and removed the defamatory articles.

This was by no means an attack on freedom of the press or legitimate journalism. On the contrary, it was a blow struck for protection of the truth in journalism by revealing the truth about online libel. It was a dollars-and-cents statement that defamation will not be tolerated. This is essential, because dollars-and-cents statements are the only kind that the perpetrators understand.

The lawsuit was a victory for the inventor of email, but more importantly it established the truth that innovation, small or large, can occur anytime, anyplace, by anybody. This is not only an important quality of the American Dream. It is a basic fact about how innovation happens.

If I can do it, you can do it, and you should do it. How to do it -- practical advice on how you can become a successful innovator -- is the subject of Part Three.

Part Four

Innovation Anywhere by Anybody

Chapter Seventeen

Seven Secrets of Innovation

We are not robots, which automatically run programs. As human beings, we are expressions of divine innovation, which we must continue through innovations of our own. I believe this is both a sacred duty and an immense opportunity. We are creations, and we should be creators as well.

Toward that end, I want to offer practical methods -- Seven Secrets of Innovation -- that I've learned over the course of my journey. These are practical, down to earth tools. They are "secrets" because, for far too long, these foundational elements have been deliberately hidden by "experts," "scholars," and "historians," many of whom serve the vested interests of a multi-trillion dollar innovation industry that wishes to perpetuate propaganda that innovation can only occur in Silicon Valley and the military. Or perhaps by dropouts, but from Elite universities.

These suppressors and oppressors, committed to a new caste system, seem incapable of accepting the fact that a 14-year-old, lower caste, Indian immigrant boy, working in Newark, New Jersey, invented email.

For them, those facts do not compute. However, the 14-year-old boy's journey reveals a fundamental truth: innovation can occur anytime, anyplace by anybody, and shatters false narratives and exposes their brainwashing, which attempt to bind the source of great innovations, such as email, within their "golden triangle" of the military, big corporations, and large universities.

These same members of the Establishment --- the Elites – perpetuate the narrative that they "know better." My journey, however, teaches me "you know better." Each one of us is a spark of divinity and intelligence, which is decentralized across every quantum of this grand Universe.

Most academics, lawyers and career politicians, who seek to pursue power in government, do not adhere to Nature's Law but think they are the only enlightened ones and the rest of us are stupid. More maliciously, these individuals, as my own journey and that of other innovators and change agents demonstrate, will go out of their way to destroy truth and ignore facts when evidence emerges contrary to their false narratives.

Secret #1

Know That Innovation Is In Your DNA

The first secret is that every human being is born to innovate. This is neither a philosophy nor a motivational statement, but a biological fact. In your DNA, are the genes for innovation. Your own denial of this fact is your road to accepting that only a few can innovate and create. More importantly, such denial leads to your own subjugation. The truth is you have nothing to lose, but your chains, by accepting the fact that innovation is your birthright.

All animals, to varying degrees, have the genetic coding for innovation. Humans, however, have this ability to a significantly larger extent. It is this genetic capability that gave us fire, irrigation, writing and email. Had I not invented email in 1978, someone else would have; however, I was the first to do it. Had J.C. Bose not invented radio, someone else would have; however, he was the first to do it, before Marconi. Had Aryabhata, not discovered the elliptical orbits of planets, someone would have (western historians deliberately record Kepler as the discoverer), but Aryabhata was the first. The destiny of humankind is to innovate, create, play and to discover the laws of the Universe, and that destiny is also encoded in your genes. What turns on those genes for innovation is the ecosystem --- the conditions that you are exposed to --- your surroundings. Modern biology, of the post-genomic era, starting around 2002, discovered a powerful new mechanism known as 42 epigenetics, which revolutionized the old and false biological theory that enslaved us to our genes. The truth is that our genes can be turned on and off by our environment. This discovery obliterates the deplorable arguments, long used to justify racism, sexism, casteism and classism, that promotes superiority of a particular race, sex, caste or class over another, based on lineage and genes. The truth is, under the right conditions, anyone can innovate, since innovation is in our DNA. For over 5,000 years, for example, Indians were innovators, creating incredible systems of healthcare (Siddha and Ayurveda), agriculture, mathematics, architecture, metallurgy, etc. However, with the brutal subjugation of Colonialism, beginning in 1657, Indians were deliberately brainwashed by their oppressor to believe that they were good for just being workers, administrators, and even high paid CEOs, for their master's bidding, but could not be in the league of innovators. That was a "Whites" only club. In 1978, my genes were turned on to invent email because I was fortunate to have been provided an incredible ecosystem of loving parents, dedicated public school teachers, and an amazing mentor, who provided me an environment, where I was given both respect and freedom to innovate, though I was only fourteen. This was long before I went to MIT, and got four degrees. As a 14-year-old, I had no sense of what was impossible. Everything was possible, and everything was play. This is why I believe young people or those with the heart and soul of a child are probably the best innovators, because their biological systems are open, flexible and resilient. They do things not for control or profit, or to make the next big company, but are compelled to do so by an inherent passion to create. So relative to this first secret, it is about your recognizing that within you is innovation. It's already encoded in your DNA.

You don't really need to attend the next big innovation seminar, or go to Harvard Business School, MIT or IIT, to learn this truth. What you need to do is to go into nature, sit still among the trees, the wind and the sun. Close your eyes and connect and realize that everything around you, and within you is innovation. You are part of that Nature. You too are imbued with Nature's fullest aspect of creativity. You are That. When you recognize this truth, you honor yourself by seeing that you too are part of that creation, and the creative power has always been with you, and you simply need to connect with that.

Secret #2

Find A Mentor

A mentor is someone who inspires you, and reminds you by their own example that you have the power to create. A mentor can be a teacher, a friend, a parent, or a stranger, may be someone you have yet to meet. They can be from any vocation: a mechanic, carpenter, artist, scientist, teacher, etc. The point is that they are someone who inspires you and can guide you in a practical way, for you to explore this important aspect of being a creative human being. In India, during ancient times, there was a teacher or "guru," not someone promoting religion or some megalomaniacal agenda, but a productive and practical member of society, who worked with you, one on one, to impart wisdom, and to lead you on a path, so you could lead yourself.

In my case, I was fortunate to have found Dr. Leslie P. Michelson. He was 20 years older than me, and there were others in the laboratory 30 to 50 years older. However, Dr. Michelson and everyone treated me as an equal, with great respect, and never was I treated as a 14-year-old kid. Dr. Michelson led by example: he worked hard, was committed to excellence, communicated effectively, and was there to give his knowledge and wisdom, and direct me to others, if and when I needed help. He was an incredible mentor. So, if you want to innovate, you must find a mentor, to set you on your path to innovation.

Secret #3

Identify A Real Problem

The third secret of innovation is to identify and solve a real problem. The problem can be big or small, but it has to be something tangible that you can clearly identify and know that if you were to solve it, it would make life easier for others. In my case, the problem I found was that secretaries, women office workers, at UMDNJ, were slaves to their typewriter and the interoffice email system. They worked endless hours writing, editing, and copying memos on a typewriter, while having to manually sort, file, archive, trash, and do many other processes, inherent to the paper based interoffice mail system. Because the system was paper-based, it was time consuming to work on that medium. For example, if they made a mistake in typing something, there was no "backspace" to easily delete the error, they had use "white out," a white paint-like liquid, to white out the mistake, wait until it dried, and only then, could they type over it. The secretary was essentially a command-and-control center for paper-based communications in each office.

The secretaries were interconnected through the interoffice mail system, very much like bees working in a honeycomb. I was able to clearly identify the problem in the interoffice mail system, and also was able to see the possibilities of how their lives could be made easier, if I could move this paper-based process to an electronic system. Because I had day-to-day interactions with these secretaries, I was able to witness hands-on the problem, and in my mind's eye, I could see the solution. So, if you want to innovate, you too must identify a tangible problem, and at least have a vision of what your solution may look like. This is essential to the process of innovation.

Secret #4

Find A Customer

The fourth, perhaps the most important secret is to find a customer! Solving a problem and finding a solution without a customer is not innovation, but is like doing a science experiment as a lonely laboratory investigator. What you create may have no tangible value to anyone. I have seen many "innovators" create things in their laboratories, and later discover that what they created is useless to the end customer. So, my biggest advice to innovators is as soon as you find a problem and conceive a solution, find a customer, with whom you can co-create the solution. In my case, my customer was the secretary. If I could help make her life easier, I not only got a customer but an ally, who would tell hundreds of other secretaries at UMDNJ how email made her job easier.

What I mean by "customer" is someone that is your partner, someone who you can co-create the solution with. Thinking you can create a solution that will miraculously be adopted, without having a customer, front and center, from the beginning, is not innovation. So, start with a customer, who will provide you immediate feedback. Many times, they will give you seemingly "dumb ideas," what may seem simpleton-like to you; however, it is precisely such dumb ideas, that can truly enhance your solution, because your customer is in real world, and their needs are very real. By addressing these needs, your solution becomes a truly valuable innovation. Remember, humans have been innovating in response to facing real problems to make the lives of others easier for over thousands of years. Innovation is ultimately about solving problems to address such needs, where human, customer interaction, is essential to the process of innovation. So, get a customer.

Secret #5

Build To Scale

The fifth secret is to recognize that while you can create an innovation for solving just your problem or just one other human being's problem, innovations that serve many, require you to build to scale. What do I mean by "build to scale?" I mean that your solution just doesn't help one customer but it helps more than one customer. Scaling means that with each new customer you help, you don't have to do many things to alter the solution to add on a new customer. If you have to change the solution each time, for every new customer, you can never "scale" the distribution of your innovation.

In my case, to invent email, I had to make sure that every secretary could use the solution. This scaling necessitated that the solution be easy-to-use. Many people don't recognize the power of making something easy-to-use. If it's easy-to-use, anyone can pick up your solution, and they can learn to use it quickly without having to read manuals, hire consultants and undergo lots of training. The more easily an individual can use your solution, the more it will be usable and can spread like wildfire. The more you need others to be involved directly with helping that one individual use your solution, you've created a barrier to your solution being utilized by many, and scaling becomes difficult. Scaling also means that your solution is cost-effective, that the pricing be fair, so people can adopt your solution with ease. In my case, with email, we charged pennies per minute of use of the email system, and this was far cheaper than typing a letter, sticking it in an envelope and paying people to transport it from office-to-office.

Scaling also is closely related to reliability, meaning that people should trust your solution. Trust helps increase adoption. In my case, we had to ensure that when the secretary selected the SEND command, on the user interface, that email arrived on time, with no errors, and at the right location.

If there were failures, they would have lost trust, would have gotten afraid, and would not have continued using my solution, particularly since they were comfortable doing something another way (paper-based) and I had wanted them to switch to a whole new way of doing things, on the computer. So, considering these aspects, during the innovation process, you can build to scale and ensure the success of your innovation.

Secret #6

Protect Your Innovation

In the modern world, one must protect the innovation. Two legal methods exist to protect your innovation: Copyright and/or Patents. Find a good legal counsel and protect your innovation as soon as possible. It is essential to ensuring the adoption, use, sale and marketing of your innovation.

We live in a legal world. Without protection of your innovation, you will not be taken seriously. In my case, when I invented email in 1978, believe it or not, there were no laws for protecting software inventions. The Copyright

Act of 1976, valid at the time, only protected music and written works, but not software. The United States Supreme Court, moreover, did not even recognize software patents. In 1980, the Copyright Act of 1976 was amended to become the Computer Software Act of 1980, which then provided a legal vehicle to protect software inventions.

As mentioned in Part One, in 1981, I was fortunate enough to attend a dinner with then MIT President Paul E. Gray. I had been invited to his home along with other class presidents, since I was the president of my freshman class. Dr. Gray was the first one who alerted me to the fact that the Supreme Court did not recognize software patents, and advised me to copyright my invention using the Computer Software Act of 1980. My parents were not lawyers and could not advise me properly. But I did follow Dr. Gray's advice and sent a letter to the U.S. Copyright Office. I received the necessary forms and submitted them. On August 30, 1982, the U.S.

government awarded me the first U.S. Copyright for "Email," officially recognizing me as the inventor of email. Today, there are many cost-effective ways to get legal advice and to protect your innovation. Literally on-line, you can file Copyrights, provisional patents, and even find patent attorneys, within minutes. It's much easier than it has ever been in history, for you to protect your innovation. Such protection is a must, and essential to the process of innovation.

Secret #7

Promote Your Innovation

Finally, the seventh secret, which I only came to learn much later on, was that one must actively promote and publicize one's innovation; or, others, those who did not invent what you did, will promote your invention, as their own, and will attempt to steal it, by owning the public's mind share. In 1978, after I invented email, I won various prestigious awards, was headlined in the local newspaper. In 1981, even MIT's main newspaper highlighted my invention. However, I did not actively hire a public relations agency to promote my invention. Remember, I was only 14-years old, and knew nothing about PR or marketing.

It was only about 35 years later, when my work was honored by the Smithsonian Institution in 2012, did I came to find out that a very large defense company, Raytheon, had spent millions of dollars promoting themselves as the "inventor of email," when in fact, what they created was not email, but a rudimentary form of text messaging, which they rebranded as "email." Raytheon deliberately misused and marketed the word "email" to refer to their work, so as to brand themselves as "innovators," in the lucrative cyber security market, where promoting that they "invented email" gave them a competitive advantage. When they came to find out that I had in fact invented email, and was asserting my rights, they unleashed the most awful vitriol using their marketing department, PR agencies and industry insiders. That was an incredible lesson for me to have learned the hard way. What's ironic is that when I attempted to share the facts, they called me self-promotional! So, learn from me, promote your innovation. Of course, make sure that you have protected it first. Since I had been fortunate to have received that advice in 1981 from Dr. Gray, MIT's president, and had officially gotten the first U.S. Copyright for Email, the facts were black and white --- a 14-year-old dark-skinned, lower-caste Indian immigrant boy, working in Newark, New Jersey, is the inventor of email. I hope these 7 secrets of innovation help you, on your journey to innovate things, be they large or small. Remember, innovation is within you. Never forget this eternal truth. I wish you all my best.

Made in the USA
Lexington, KY
13 December 2017